MW00978194

CHARACTER QUESTIONS

Karen Dockrey

MissionsQuest

Woman's Missionary Union
Birmingham, Alabama

Woman's Missionary Union
P. O. Box 830010
Birmingham, AL 35283-0010

Unless otherwise indicated, Scripture quotations are from *Contemporary English Version*. Copyright © American Bible Society 1991. Used by permission.

Scriptures identified KJV are from the King James Version of the Bible.

Cover design by Janell Young

ISBN: 1-56309-263-8
W986123•0898•2M2

CHARACTER QUESTIONS

Welcome to the world of questions. You are now old enough and wise enough to ask questions—questions that matter, questions whose answers determine the way you live your life. As you ask, put into action the answers you discover. While you live the truth, you'll understand it even better. You'll know God more thoroughly. You'll find answers to questions you didn't even know you had. You'll become a woman of character.

Let me assure you that asking questions is a sign of deep faith in God. When you ask God a question, you show you trust Him to have the answers. And because He does have the answers, you will find them. It may take days, weeks, years, even a lifetime, but the answers will come. Keep on asking. Keep on living what you discover. The contented life you discover will be worth your energy and attention.

Every time you have a question, ask God about it. Ask about God. About guys. About family. About school. About yourself. About your friends. About feelings. About worries. About the present. About the future. About your place in this world and the next. The only stupid question is one you refuse to pursue. Remember throughout your search to ask people who

1

get their answers from Jesus Christ—the only true source of real answers.

Every now and then, even in church, you'll run across people who tell you not to ask questions, or who treat your questions as a lack of faith. That's OK. They may be a little afraid of questions, or may have been mistakenly taught that questions are bad. When they say, "Just have faith," they don't realize that unquestioned faith can lead to cults and other contrary-to-Jesus religions. They don't know that honest questions lead to better understanding of God and to stronger faith. Understand, and then move to another Christian who will help you find your answers.

Again, as you find your answers, live them. Notice how and why God's truth works in real life. For example, Jesus says in Luke to do unto others as you want them to do to you. And you discover that when you talk to a guy as a person, just the way you'd want to be treated, you both feel more comfortable and happy together. The Book of Proverbs says a gentle answer turns away wrath. You notice that when you respond calmly, your parents treat you much more like an adult. God's ways really do work.

Keep asking. Keep putting into practice. Keep showing what you believe and why. This is the process of becoming a person of character.

WHAT IS CHARACTER?

I'm glad you asked. It's the first question to move you onward in your quest to be a woman of godly character.

Character is your personality . . .

Character is how people describe you . . .

Character is your choices . . .

Character is the friendships you build with both guys and girls . . .

Character is your attitudes and tones . . .

Character is how you spend your time . . .

Character is how you act when no one is looking . . .

Character is how you get along with the people who others say don't matter . . .

Character is how you manage your relationships and commitments . . .

Character is all this and more. It's everything you do, think, and say. To choose the character you want, discover just the way God wants you to live out your commitment to Him in everyday life.

Who do you want to be? How do you want your life to count? What do you want people to say about you? Ask these questions and more to grow godly character. Find these answers and more in God's Holy Word, the Bible.

You've spent a delightful year discovering what godly character is and how to display it. You've asked

God to show you truth and He has. I encourage you to keep asking about character and discovering how to live it. I invite you to continue your quest for character, even as you live what you've already discovered. Let your character both ask questions and answer them:

How can I grow Christlike character?

> *I grow Christlike by imitating Jesus.*

Can I change my character?

> *I have power to change because of Jesus.*

Why do I have trouble doing the good I want to do and avoiding bad even when I know it's wrong?

> *Because all believers struggle (see Rom. 7:15–8:2).*

Why can't I handle life better?

> *Because life is hard. I just need solutions and strategies.*

This devotional guide is designed to give you just the solutions and strategies you need to live your faith as a woman of godly character. But devotionals can't do it all for you. Other places to go to ask questions and to learn how to be a Christian of character include:
•The Bible;
•Christian parents;
•Christian grandparents;
•Christian music (evaluate it—some tells the truth, some does not);

4

- Christian magazines;
- Adults who live their faith daily;
- God Himself.

God will be the One Who will answer your questions whether it be through a prayer, a person, a printed piece, or an experience. He is always there, always listening, always eager to help you understand, always powerful enough to equip you to put into practice good and godly character.

"Ask, and you will receive.
Seek, and you will find.
Knock, and the door will be opened for you"
(Matt. 7:7).

WHERE CAN I FIND CONFIDENCE?

"You can be sure that the Lord will protect you from harm" (Prov. 3:26).

DAY 1: WHY ARE SOME PEOPLE SO NATURALLY CONFIDENT?

Some people seem born with confidence. They enter this world with a persistence that moves past all obstacles to find good. But most of us must learn confidence. The people around us show how to work patiently for what we want. They remind us why we're here and how deeply we're loved. This unbeatable combination of "you're worth this," and "you can do this," grows confidence.

These investments people make in you are called love. Love originates with God and when people don't block it, love comes directly into your life. The Bible says it like this:

"You have accepted Christ Jesus as your Lord. Now keep on following him. Plant your roots in Christ and let him be the foundation of your life. Be strong in your faith, just as you were taught. And be grateful" (Col. 2:6–7).

Perhaps you were born to parents who chose to grow roots in you. They applauded your first attempts to climb in that chair or sound out that word. When you struggled with math they got out the blocks and let you count them until you understood subtraction. The pie you had for dinner helped you understand fractions. Even if you didn't have parents who took the time to show you how and why to live life, God has placed other adults in your life. Teachers. Employers. Friends at church. Authors who write to you even before they meet you. Watch and learn from the God-given people around you.

Then imitate them by investing in others, by passing on what you know. Say to your sister or acquaintance, "You can do that algebra problem. Here, I'll show you."

"If you fall, your friend can help you up. But if you fall without having a friend nearby, you are really in trouble" (Eccl. 4:10).

DAY 2: SO HOW DO I GAIN CONFIDENCE?

Confidence is something you grow and nurture, not something you find full-grown. It happens as you choose to do the right thing and see the good that results. Each time you resist a temptation and see the power that comes in being true to God, you grow confidence. Each time you value people over position, you grow confidence. Each time you work first and then play, you grow confidence. Each time you choose to spend your time well, you grow confidence. The Bible says it like this:

"Honesty and justice will prosper there, and justice will produce lasting peace and security" (Isa. 32:16,17).

Confidence grows with each righteous action, each righteous word, each righteous attitude. To be righteous is to do right by God's standards. It's not talking like a monk or saying holy-sounding words or going to church all the time. It's basing your actions on love for God and your relationship with Him. It's treating people the way God would. It's spending time the way Jesus would. It's valuing what the Holy Spirit values.

Righteousness is justice, fairness, love, and honor. It's being tough enough to do right no matter how embarrassed you feel. It's being soft enough to show love even when it means you feel sappy.

Deliberately choose to do good, love well, and live in honor of the God Who is on your side. As you do, your confidence will grow so powerfully that you don't have to prove yourself, doubt yourself, or betray yourself.

"Keep on being brave! It will bring you great rewards" (Heb. 10:35).

DAY 3: WHY DO SOME PEOPLE SQUASH MY CONFIDENCE?

Even when you let God give you confidence, people will challenge you. It happened to a believing king named Hezekiah hundreds of years ago. His people faced Assyria, a cruel and oppressive nation:

"Then, in a voice loud enough for everyone to hear, he shouted out in Hebrew: 'Listen to what the great king of Assyria says! Don't be fooled by Hezekiah. He can't save you. Don't trust him when he tells you that the Lord will protect you from the king of Assyria. . . . Were there any other gods able to defend their land against the king of Assyria?'" (Isa. 36:13–15,18b).

This Assyrian commander was a master at instilling doubt and fear, even among the faithful. People with the same ability will cross your path. They may not use words, but the effect can be just as depressing:

•Perhaps it's someone with popularity who invites votes no matter how badly he treats people;

•Perhaps it's a girl with looks that turn guys' eyes and make you feel like a potato sack;

•Perhaps it's another believer who slips you ugly barbs from the side when adult leaders aren't listening.

In each case you can overcome the discouraging comments to go ahead and do the right action anyway.

How? Through the power of Almighty God. Admit to Him your pain and frustration. Let Him hug you and assure you of your worth. Then one step at a time, do the right thing.

"Be brave and strong! . . . The Lord your God will always be at your side, and he will never abandon you" (Deut. 31:6).

DAY 4: WHAT IF I DON'T FEEL CONFIDENT?

Confidence is not a feeling as much as an action. It's going ahead and doing what needs doing, no matter how scared or shy you feel. Most feelings of confidence come *after* the fact, not before. So go ahead and:

•speak to the person you want to meet;

•try the skill you want to master;

•apply for the job you really want and tell the manager why you want it;

•give the person next to you confidence with a "you can do it";

•say the good you see even if no one else sees it;

•get your work done first so you can really enjoy your free time;

•invite people to join you for the activity you want to do.

God Himself will equip you to do well and to do right. And with each good choice you'll shoot out one more root of stability. Then you will always have confidence to do the right thing, whether times are easy or hard, whether you're tired or rested, whether you're alone or with a crowd of caring people. The Bible says it like this:

"But I will bless those who trust in me. They will be like trees growing beside a stream—trees with roots that reach down to the water, and with leaves that are always green. They bear fruit every year and are never worried by a lack of grain" (Jer. 17:7–8).

You are like a tree planted by the water because God will always provide confidence, words, and care from which to draw.

"I've commanded you to be strong and brave. Don't ever be afraid or discouraged! I am the Lord your God, and I will be there to help you wherever you go" (Josh. 1:9).

DAY 5: HOW CAN I BOOST
THE CONFIDENCE OF OTHERS?

You are a power source. Simply by speaking words of confidence to people, you give them confidence. The Bible calls this encouragement. As you speak encouraging words you become a vehicle God uses to help people recognize and live the good He created in them. So use words that remind people that God cares, that they can honor Him, that they are worth doing the right thing. Notice the confidence-giving power God gives through words like:

"You can do it."	*rather than*	"Don't blow it."
"Everybody makes mistakes."	*rather than*	"How could you be so stupid?"
"I like the way you did that."	*rather than*	"Why can't you do it this way?"
"That's a great idea."	*rather than*	"It'll never work."
"Thanks for being my friend."	*rather than*	keeping quiet.
"What you said really helped."	*rather than*	assuming she just knows.

16

Each of your words will either make someone feel better about God and life, or worse. So give confidence to those around you by letting God love through your words. Be a living vessel of His grace, saying words He would say to encourage friends as He would do. This is your goal:

"Christ now gives us courage and confidence, so that we can come to God by faith. . . . I kneel in prayer to the Father. . . . God is wonderful and glorious. I pray that his Spirit will make you become strong followers" (Eph. 3:12,14,16).

Perhaps just as important, find friends who will give you the same encouragement and confidence. Understand each other. Prompt each other to do good. Bring out the best in each other.

"Encourage anyone who feels left out, help all who are weak, and be patient with everyone" (1 Thess. 5:14*b*).

2

WHERE DOES LOVE FIT IN?

"We love because God loved us first"
(1 John 4:19).

DAY 1: WHY DOES LOVE MATTER?

Love matters because love is the foundation for everything we do. We seek it, offer it, fear we'll never receive it. The good news is that God has given love to each of us so completely that we can seek, offer, and receive with tremendous delight. Love is the basis of every character trait:

Love gives confidence to bridge relationships;

Love provides the courage to do the right thing for the right reason;

Love inspires creative use of time, skills, money, and the brain;

Love gives a reason to show true character;

Love prompts you to settle for no less than excellence;

Love offers vision of what can be, so you work to bring it to reality.

Love is not the found-only-in-storybooks kind of gushy feeling. It's the much longer lasting commitment to companionship. Companionship is togetherness. This includes togetherness with God, togetherness with friends, togetherness between guys and girls. The Bible describes it like this:

"Love is kind and patient, never jealous, boastful, proud, or rude. Love isn't selfish or quick tempered. It doesn't keep a record of wrongs that others do. Love rejoices in the truth, but not in evil" (1 Cor. 13:4–6).

Notice that each of these qualities is a decision, not a feeling. True love chooses to care even when it's rough. The feelings follow the decision. The decisions can't be based on feelings. Love is friendship at its best.

"My dear friends, we must love each other. Love comes from God, and when we love each other, it shows we have been given new life" (1 John 4:7a).

DAY 2: HOW DOES MY FAMILY IMPACT LOVE?

Learning how to love begins at home. If you watch your parents hear and understand each other, working together on all endeavors, you tend to show romance in these love-building ways. But if you've seen power plays, misunderstandings, and defensiveness, you assume that's the nature of guy-girl relationships. Or you declare that your relationship will be totally different with no struggles, divorces, or in-home splits, only to repeat the same frustrating patterns.

Are you doomed to repeat whatever bad patterns your parents formed? Not at all. You can grow new patterns. Notice what matches God's plan for love and imitate that. Deliberately change the nonmatches, conscious that it will be a continual, but fruitful, struggle. Choose to grow a love like this:

"What if I could speak all languages of humans and angels? If I did not love others, I would be nothing more than a noisy gong or a clanging cymbal. What if I could prophesy and understand all secrets and all knowledge? And what if I had faith that moved mountains? I would be nothing unless I loved others. What if I gave away all that I owned and let myself be burned alive? I would gain nothing, unless I loved others" (1 Cor. 13:1–3).

No matter how romantically a guy talks, if he doesn't considerately hear your ideas, his romance is useless. If he's brilliant in school or in his knowledge of the Bible, but doesn't show respect for you and your friends, there's not enough love to last a lifetime. If he goes on missions trips and donates lots of money but can't treat his own family and friends well, his love is cancelled out. Settle for nothing less than building the real thing.

"Love is always supportive, loyal, hopeful, and trusting. Love never fails!" (1 Cor. 13:7–8*a*).

DAY 3: WHY LOVE MY FRIENDS?

Your friends are more than the people you spend time with; they're your life-teachers. As such they help you learn how to love, or keep you from true love. Together you discover what guys are like, which adults are worth trusting, and how to love each other as friends. So choose well.

The best friends see the good God created in you and make it easier for you to show it. Spend the most time with people who free you to be your best self, who make it easy for you to laugh, who appreciate you when you treat people well, who encourage you to trust your God and yourself. Watch for friends who live their faith, not just those who wear the label *Christian*. What qualities shall you avoid and seek according to this Bible passage?

"The poor are ruled by the rich, and those who borrow are slaves of moneylenders. Troublemakers get in trouble, and their terrible anger will get them nowhere. The Lord blesses everyone who freely gives food to the poor. Arguments and fights will come to an end, if you chase away those who insult others. The king is the friend of all who are sincere and speak with kindness" (Prov. 22:7–11).

Avoid all hints of defensiveness, possessiveness, secretiveness, or deceptiveness in your friendships.

Instead seek delight, fascination with life, love for all persons, and devotion to learning (not just from books but from every source). A friend who grows alongside you is perhaps the best of all. Then when romance comes along you can truly be happy for one another.

"Live in harmony by showing love for each other. Be united in what you think, as if you were only one person. Don't be jealous or proud, but be humble and consider others more important than yourselves. Care about them as much as you care about yourselves and think the same way that Christ Jesus thought" (Phil. 2:2b–5).

DAY 4: HOW CAN I MEET GUYS?

There's always been something intriguing about guys, but recently you've grown more interested in the one-to-one partnership God calls marriage. You don't want to walk the aisle this year, but you do want to find that kindred spirit, a guy you can share life with—everything from doing homework together to exchanging gifts at Christmas. You want someone who understands you, knows and likes you, and who enjoys being with you. You want love.

But somewhere between the want to and what we do, things get skewed. Too many of us ignore the faith factor and focus on emotion, or settle for people who treat us badly. Or we don't tell how we really feel and the person never knows the real us. Why can't we grow real love?

The answers are complex, but they begin with self-lessness—see guys as people first. Turn outside yourself to honestly care what they think, dream, and feel. Selflessly take the risk of revealing your thoughts, dreams, and feelings. Selfless love is willing to be cheesy enough to voice your care and willing to risk enough to show your real self. It's good and right, and deeply based in Jesus. You can do it because God will equip you: "I know what it is to be poor or to have plenty, and I have lived under all kinds of conditions. I know what it means to be full or to be hungry, to have too much or too little. Christ gives me the strength to face anything" (Phil. 4:12–13).

Like guys as people first, growing closest to the ones who also honor Jesus in their daily walk. Guys who are good friends are some of the best picks for dating. Why? Because marriage is first and best a friendship.

"God loves people who love to give" (2 Cor. 9:7*b*).

DAY 5: WHAT IF I DON'T FEEL LIKE LOVING?

This is the true test of love—to choose to love when you don't feel like it:

•You were up late studying for an exam and your just-home-from-a-wild-day mom asks you to unload the dishwasher while she cooks dinner. You patiently do it with the same time you would have protested. As you work, share with her how the exam went.
•You're upset because the test you studied for was different than you expected and your night of study didn't help much. Your brother asks for math help. Kindly show him how to do the problems so he will have a better day at school than you did.
•You're so excited about the letter that came in the mail, but your Dad also has great news. Take turns talking.

How do you do all this? Think of how it would make you feel. And recognize that the way you treat people shows your love for Jesus:
"Then the ones who pleased the Lord will ask, 'When did we give you something to eat or drink? When did we welcome you as a stranger or give you clothes to wear or visit you while you were sick or in jail?' The king will answer, 'Whenever you did it for any of my

people, no matter how unimportant they seemed, you did it for me'" (Matt. 25:37–40).

As you practice treating your family members with love, you'll build habits that will equip you for love in marriage.

"Show love in everything you do" (1 Cor. 16:14).

3

WHERE'S COURAGE WHEN I NEED IT?

"Christ gives me the strength
to face anything"
(Phil. 4:13).

DAY 1: HOW CAN I FIND COURAGE TO BE MYSELF?

Discovering your best self is a process. You venture out to see what you do well and how to do so even better. This happens best when surrounded by a loving family, caring friends, and a church who lives the Bible rather than just talks about it. These people see your good, highlight it, and show you how to live it. Because this world is imperfect, most of us don't have all of this. So look for the good folks God sends to see and encourage the good in you. Perhaps your dad consistently points out your strong points. Maybe there's one friend among a sea of critics who always loves to hear what you have to say. Let these people give you courage to live and to love. Then be that person to others:

"God is love. If we keep on loving others, we will stay one in our hearts with God, and he will stay one with us. If we truly love others and live as Christ did in this world, we won't be worried about the day of judgment. A real love for others will chase those worries away. The thought of being punished is what makes us afraid. It shows that we have not really learned to love" (1 John 4:16–18).

Courageously living and loving are skills. They grow more complete with each action. Each time you ask a question that prompts someone to talk, you drive out the fear of loneliness. Every time you listen, you drive out a person's fear that her comments make no sense. Every time you compliment positively, you drive out the fear of being put down. Courage takes the place of fear. Security nestles in. Good grows.

"You can be sure that the Lord will protect you from harm" (Prov. 3:26).

DAY 2: WHAT IF I DON'T FEEL BRAVE?

Courage is an action, not a feeling. You look fear in the face and remind it who is boss. Because Jesus Christ has equipped you to manage fear, you can face it. You never face fear alone, you face it together with Christ.

Facing fear is seldom easy, even when you're God. Jesus, God in human form, prayed all night getting ready for His crucifixion. He knew the nails would hurt. He knew the mocking would be humiliating. He prayed and let angels minister to Him. Even then it was agonizing. That's OK. What matters is He went ahead and faced the experience:

"Jesus . . . knelt down and prayed. 'Father, if you will, please don't make me suffer by having me drink from this cup. But do what you want, and not what I want.' Then an angel from heaven came to help him. Jesus was in great pain and prayed so sincerely that his sweat fell to the ground like drops of blood" (Luke 22:41–44).

Facing fear is easier when you have a reason. Jesus faced the crucifixion to show us how deeply He loved us. You might face your fear of ridicule to stand up for a friend who's being unfairly treated. You gain not only the friend you defend but those who watch. They know they can trust you.

You might face your fear of failure to speak up in class. You gain not only the teacher's approval but greater enjoyment of class discussion. You also find ways to speak the truth for Jesus' sake.

"Armies may surround me, but I won't be afraid; war may break out, but I will trust you" (Psalm 27:3).

DAY 3: WILL I ALWAYS BE AFRAID?

There's a lot to fear in this world. Death. Violence. Betrayal. Loneliness. Illness. Abandonment. Loss. Confusion. It's enough to make you give up. But don't. Courageously walk past these to the good on the other side.

Begin by understanding the hows and whys. These bad things don't come from God. They're not His nature. Most of these bad things come from human choice—people choose to betray, abandon, deceive, and hurt. Other bad things come from this imperfect world—cancer in a child and the eventual death of every human, no matter how healthy he or she may be. All of it makes God sad. So He determines not to let bad things have the last word.

God offers something better: the certainty that He will one day wipe away all these bad things, all these events that work against Him and His life, kindness, loyalty, togetherness, health, gain, and understanding. We will one day be with Him and be totally secure: "He will live with them, and they will be his own. Yes, God will make his home among his people. He will wipe all tears from their eyes, and there will be no more death, suffering, crying or pain. These things of the past are gone forever" (Rev. 21:3*b*–4).

Until then there will be troubles. There will be pain. But that's not all there will be. If we choose it, and if we find others who are choosing it, we can experience right now a hint of God's life, kindness, loyalty, togetherness, health, gain, and understanding. We can let these good experiences give us reason to courageously walk on through the bad ones.

"You, Lord, are the light that keeps me safe. I am not afraid of anyone. You protect me, and I have no fears" (Psalm 27:1).

DAY 4: HOW CAN I GIVE COURAGE TO MY FRIENDS?

It's the little things that count. Do you have courage to ask your questions so you can quit agonizing over them? Will you take the risk to talk with the guy you want to get to know so you gain his friendship and discover that he has admired you but didn't know how to approach you? Will you make your own tough choices so no one else has to boss you around? Can you stay loyal through easy and hard times?

All these are easier with a friend. And you have two of them. One is Jesus Christ. He came to live on earth and followed all the rules you follow. He knows just what to do about the sticky problems because He faced them:

"We have a great high priest, who has gone into heaven, and he is Jesus the Son of God. That is why we must hold on to what we have said about him. Jesus understands every weakness of ours, because he was tempted in every way that we are. But he did not sin! So whenever we are in need, we should come bravely before the throne of our merciful God. There we will be treated with undeserved kindness, and we will find help" (Heb. 4:14–16).

Your other friend is any person you choose to share courage with. Maybe you unselfconsciously explore a

toy store just to enjoy childhood again. Or you take
the time to befriend the new girl. Or you can sit beside
a boy who can't hear to take notes for him. Together
you can courageously do right. It's called fellowship.

*"God blesses those people who want to obey him more than
to eat or drink. They will be given what they want!"*
(Matt. 5:6).

DAY 5: WHY DOES COURAGE MATTER, ANYWAY?

Courage enables you to overcome the popularity ranking at your school to see the person under the label. Courage equips you to treat people well for the right reasons. Courage grows the right kind of "I don't care what people think about me." You're then free to make friends with every person, confident that true popularity is borne of genuine care, not shallow rankings.

Courage is the ability to look in the mirror and like what you see, to realize that liking yourself honors God. You know that smiles and sincerity are much more attractive than makeup and status clothes. You're not conceited. Conceit is borne of bragging. You have true love for self, the freedom to love other people.

Courage gives you the gumption to take school so seriously that you don't worry about being called a nerd. You worry more about learning than grades, and you see every experience as an opportunity to discover more about life and people. You build a balanced life that takes as much pride in work as in pleasure. The Bible says it like this:

"Don't fall in love with money. Be satisfied with what you have. The Lord has promised that he will not leave us or desert us. That should make you feel like saying,

'The Lord helps me! Why should I be afraid of what people can do to me?'" (Heb. 13:5–6).

Invite God to give you a passion for right that is so powerful that you'll plow through or poke past any obstacle. Then delight in loving people, loving yourself, and loving your work with the passion of God Himself.

"The Lord is disgusted with all who do wrong, but he loves everyone who does right" (Prov. 15:9).

4

WHERE ARE THE LASTING FRIENDSHIPS?

"Some friends don't help, but a true friend is closer than your own family" (Prov. 18:24).

DAY 1: WHY CAN'T I JUST GO AHEAD AND TALK?

You know the truths—the best way to have a friend is to be one, take initiative, and friendships take time to grow. But still you hesitate. Why can't you just go ahead and talk to people?

Because it's scary.

You might get rejected.

They might think you're weird.

Friendships have risks. The one you talk to might not talk back. Or she might control you rather than like you. Or she might be so different that you don't have any fun together.

Friendships also have potential rewards. She might delight in what you say. The two of you might already like the same things and understand just how the other feels. You might grow more alike with each time you spend together. You might give each other courage to do and say the right thing at the right time. You might grow the friendship described in these Bible verses:

"A friend is always a friend, and relatives are born to share our troubles" (Prov. 17:17).

"When others are happy, be happy with them, and when they are sad, be sad" (Rom. 12:15).

Let the potential benefits outweigh the risks. How? By letting Jesus give you courage and words. Talk to

Jesus inside your head as a potential friend approaches you in the hall, as you say that first tenuous hello, as you ask a question, and as you get to know each other. Jesus lived on earth, and so He knows just how to do friendship. He'll help you every step of the way.

"The Word became a human being and lived here with us" (John 1:14*a*).

DAY 2: WHOM SHOULD I PICK FOR FRIENDS?

"Some friends don't help," says Proverbs 18:24. "A friend to all is a friend to none," says an English proverb. These sayings don't mean to be snobby, but to choose friends according to character. Delightful life-sharing won't happen with everyone you meet:
•Some people are more interested in using you than loving you;
•Other people do all the taking and none of the giving;
•Still others choose values that work in direct opposition to God;
•And others bring out the worst in you.

But delightful life-sharing can happen. Choose friends willing to do this sharing with you. Why? Because you'll become just like your friends. Why else? Because people who care about people are much more fun to be around. You won't always recognize right away if a friend is good for you. But notice qualities like contentment, the ability to have fun without hurting anyone, commitment to school and work, and family appreciation. Pull away from those without these qualities, and spend more time with those who have them. Proverbs 18:24 also says, "a true friend is closer than your own family."

Find friends who, like good family members, will share both the easy and hard times of life with you; who will tell you the honest truth that may sting at first, but will give you confidence to pull away from the hurtful path you were walking on; who will admit it when they're hurting rather than cover up with "everything's OK." Such genuine sharing of what matters is a rare treat, well worth mining for. Then be that kind of friend to others.

"The way in which you have proved yourselves by this service will bring honor and praise to God. You believed the message about Christ, and you obeyed it by sharing generously with God's people and with everyone else" (2 Cor. 9:13).

DAY 3: HOW DO I BRING OUT THE GOOD IN MY FRIENDS?

Laura has it. She has the genuine care that enjoys life without worrying about what others think. Her "I don't care" is said without a hint of rebellion and with a generous supply of security. She worries less about doing what's popular and more about doing what's genuinely fun. If she wants to spend an afternoon playing the games she treasured as a child, she'll do so. If she wants to stay up all night on a Friday night just talking with her friend, she'll do so. If she wants to hug her mom or tease another adult, she does so with unselfconscious joy.

Laura and her friend help each other refuse to worry about what people say—because no matter what they do, someone will criticize it. So they worry more about enjoying life, about enjoying each other, and about giving each other advice that will make a genuine difference. They walk in love:

"Do as God does. After all, you are his dear children. Let love be your guide. Christ loved us and offered his life for us as a sacrifice that pleases God. You are God's people, so don't let it be said that any of you are immoral or indecent or greedy. Instead, say how thankful you are. Don't let anyone trick you with foolish talk. God punishes anyone who disobeys him and says foolish things" (Eph. 5:1–4,6).

Friendship is meant to give us the connections that prompt us to be who God wants us to be. Laura and her friend do exactly that with a joy and laughter that are simply contagious.

"Always be glad because of the Lord! I will say it again: Be glad" (Phil. 4:4).

DAY 4: WHAT IF MY FRIENDS TURN UGLY?

Especially in middle school, friends can turn ugly and mean. Some never get over it. They worry so much about acceptance that they stomp all over you on their path to popularity. This hurts deeply.

And it's confusing. Why would someone you had great times with in elementary school turn on you? Doesn't what you had count for anything? Why would someone who talks about loving God treat people so pitifully? Don't they see that money and popularity won't like them back? Why doesn't God do something?

He does. But not all friends are willing to listen. They prefer the call of status to the call of friendship. The saddest part is the love they seek in status has been offered by the very people they push aside to get to it. So they stay lonely, push harder for status, and grow meaner with each push to the top.

What can you do about it? You can turn to the Friend Who doesn't turn on you, the Friend Who has lived here and has felt the sting of rejection, God Himself in the person Jesus Christ. Let Him hold you as you cry:

"My friends have rejected me, but God is the one I beg" (Job 16:20).

"My most trusted friend has turned against me, though he ate at my table" (Psalm 41:9).

Then turn to people with skin on them—the other friends God provides to give you the love you lost. Shed bitterness each time it comes. Talk about the anger and hurt you feel. But spend the most time with real friends who really care throughout real life.

"Stop being bitter and angry and mad at others. . . . Instead, be kind and merciful, and forgive others, just as God forgave you because of Christ" (Eph. 4:31a,32).

DAY 5: WHO IS MY FOUNDATION FRIEND?

As I went off to college, the support systems I was accustomed to were far away—my parents, my high school teachers, adult friends at church. Midway through my first year my beloved grandfather died. What was I to do?

I turned to the other people God brought my way. God not only gave me telephone contact with the people I already depended on—family and friends back home—but new friends who met the same needs. They listened to my exciting news. They asked questions that helped me think through decisions. They cheered me on when a test was coming. They cared about my spiritual growth. They didn't take the place of other family and friends; but they met the same needs.

This experience demonstrated for me a very real truth:
"I pray that God will take care of all your needs with the wonderful blessings that come from Christ Jesus!" (Phil. 4:19).

God met my needs through real people. I discovered that no matter what happened, whether moving away from family I loved or losing a family member by death, God would always be there to fill the gap with those who could take care of me. Never in quite the same way, but always with the love and at-homeness I needed.

I discovered that I was secure. Not through money, or position, or even family, but through an eternal God Who would always and everywhere take care of me. That same security is yours for the asking.

"I am the Lord, your God, the Holy One of Israel, the God who saves you. . . . To me, you are very dear, and I love you" (Isa. 43:3a,4a).

5

WHAT IF I'M NOT CREATIVE?

"IN THE BEGINNING GOD CREATED
THE HEAVENS AND THE EARTH. . . .
GOD LOOKED AT WHAT HE HAD DONE.
ALL OF IT WAS VERY GOOD!" (GEN. 1:1,31a).

DAY 1: HOW CAN I BE CREATIVE?

Ultimately only God is creative, because only God creates out of nothing. But because you are created in God's image, you can be creative. Invite God to bring out in you the creativity He has put there. The Bible pictures it like this:

"Every time I think of you, I thank my God. . . . This is because you have taken part with me in spreading the good news from the first day you heard about it. God is the one who began this good work in you, and I am certain that he won't stop before it is complete on the day that Christ Jesus returns" (Phil. 1:3,5–6).

Because God is not finished with people yet, you can offer yourself as a worker in His creative efforts. Take the resources God provides and bring good, conscious that every creative thing you do is in partnership with God. Ways to be creative include:

•Seeing people as being under construction. Choose to use encouraging words to prompt people to see the good God is creating in them daily, words like "You are such a good friend to people. Keep up the good loving."

•Seeing relationships as something to create. Say words and do actions that make your family relationships stronger instead of more strained, words like, "How was your day, Mom?"

•Seeing schoolwork as a creative process of learning. Look at assignments from a new angle. Rather than "I've got a vocabulary assignment," think "Some of these words might be useful in the story I'm writing. I wonder what they mean?"
•Seeing songs and paintings as pictures of God's good. Write, draw, or doodle a truth you see.

Be creative not because you are talented but because you are like God, through Jesus Christ.

"So God created humans to be like himself" (Gen. 1:27*a*).

DAY 2: WHAT IF I CAN'T DRAW?

Drawing and other visual arts are only a few forms of creativity. Notice the creativity in:

Letter writing. What can you say with your words or doodles that communicates God's love and your love for the one to whom you're writing? How do your words invite the reader to believe the good God has created in her or him?

Plants. How do you cultivate violets or vegetables in ways that bring joy to people? Perhaps your flowers help someone recognize that they make a difference. Or your vegetables help nourish someone after a horrible illness.

Conversation. How do your questions and expressions invite people to say what's really on their minds rather than the standard "fine, thank you"?

Family. How do your actions and words make each parent and sibling feel a treasured part of the unit? How do you appreciate the things each does for the other such as chores, money-earning, or homework help?

*Are you good at fixing things? Baking? Decorating? Writing stories? Composing songs? Asking good questions? More?

Treasure the gifts of creativity God has given you. In whatever way you create, move past the faulty values of this world to find and care for what really matters. The Bible says it like this:

"You were told . . . that you must give up your old way of life with all its bad habits. Let the Spirit change your way of thinking and make you into a new person. You were created to be like God, and so you must please him and be truly holy" (Eph. 4:22–25).

"Don't be like the people of this world, but let God change the way you think. Then you will know how to do everything that is good and pleasing to him" (Rom. 12:2).

DAY 3: HOW CAN I TELL TRUE CREATIVITY?

Artists are known for bickering over what art is. Genesis 1:31 describes true creativity—it is very good. *Good* includes right, pure, complete, and as it should be. How does your work show more of what life should be? How does it communicate real feelings about real events that really matter? How does it invite people to be their best? How does it treat people as never-to-be-repeated treasures?

Let all you do encourage people to partake in real living. The Bible describes how one believer invited God to do this:

"But you want complete honesty, so teach me true wisdom. . . . Let me be happy and joyful! You crushed my bones, now let them celebrate. . . . Create pure thoughts in me and make me faithful again. . . . Make me as happy as you did when you saved me; and make me want to obey!" (Psalm 51:6,8,10,12).

You, of course, cannot forgive, cleanse someone's spirit, or restore the joy of salvation. That's God's job. But you can make it easier for a friend or acquaintance to receive these gifts. How? By making church a happy place to be. And by acting like a believer wherever you go.

Creatively welcome people at church by inviting them to sit with you, by telling two people what they both like as you introduce them: "You both like cooking. I've eaten some of your desserts, Kali, and your soups, Jason." Highlight the wise things people say in Bible study, whether those people have been a part of the group for one week or several years. Be honest, caring, and affirming.

Then do these same things outside the church building.

"Kindness is rewarded" (Prov. 11:17).

DAY 4: WHAT IS WORD CREATIVITY?

Perhaps one of the best ways to be creative is in the way you use your words. Every word you say can bring a person closer to the way God is creating them. You can give encouragement with your words, assure people they are loved, notice the good they are doing, give an idea that helps them with a current challenge, ask a question that helps them solve a problem, and argue amiably. See your words as one of the most creative—or destructive—powers at your disposal. Then deliberately use them positively. The Bible says it like this:

"Stop all your dirty talk. Say the right thing at the right time and help others by what you say" (Eph. 4:29).

Notice what your friend or family needs, not just wants, and provide that. Does she need attention? Advice? Hope? Help? Ideas? Appreciation? A listening ear?

The timing and tone of your words is just as important as the words you choose. You can grow back a love that has fizzled simply with well-timed words and an interested tone. You can solve problems by using your words to apologize and find the solution. Start right where you are to use your words to create along with God. Ask questions like these to start:

Does what you say encourage people, or make them feel defeated?

Do you mean what you say, or do you lie to get what you want?

Do your words use people or love people?

Do you let every word out of your mouth do good for God?

"Try hard to do right, and you will win friends" (Prov. 11:27a).

DAY 5: HOW DOES CREATIVITY SOLVE PROBLEMS?

Resourcefulness. It's a word used to describe someone with creative ways of solving everyday problems. A group of children are bored while at a family gathering of adults. One adult excuses himself from the table, goes outside, fires up the engine on an old tractor, and takes the children for rides. The whole group comes out to watch and enjoy. That's resourcefulness—helping everyone have a good time.

A busload of excited teenagers departs for a youth retreat. One fellow is hard-of-hearing and depends on lipreading to understand conversations. A counselor breaks out penlights for every youth group member and makes a game of talking only with a flashlight on the face. Few realize that the purpose of the game is to unselfconsciously allow the deaf member to participate. That's resourcefulness.

A dedicated-to-God teenager wants to read her Bible daily but finds herself at the end of each day without having done it. She finally assigns it to herself as homework and does it along with her other assignments. She has a successful quiet time every school day. That's resourcefulness.

Creatively handle the stuff of life with solutions that work. It's where the water hits the wheel; it's faith in action. The Bible says it like this:

"Listen, Israel! The Lord our God is the only true God! So love the Lord your God with all your heart, soul, and strength. Memorize his laws and tell them to your children over and over again. Talk about them all the time, whether you're at home or walking along the road or going to bed at night, or getting up in the morning" (Deut. 6:4–7).

"Live right, and you will eat from the life-giving tree. And if you act wisely, others will follow" (Prov. 11:30).

6

WHAT CHARACTER DO I WANT?

"You are respected by everyone in town"
(Ruth 3:11).

DAY 1: WHY DOES CHARACTER MATTER?

Ultimately you reflect on you. Like Ruth of the Old Testament, it was her actions more than her words that showed her commitment to doing right for people and to people. People watch you the same way. You can show your character just as Ruth did.

Ruth was from outside the accepted group, but she proved herself and was accepted. She was the daughter-in-law of a community member, but it was her own actions that won her the respect of people around her. You are at the same point in life. You may come from a fine Christian family, but it is your actions that determine your character. You may have no one who encourages you in faith, but you can still choose to be a woman of character. You can do the right thing at the right time for the right reason. The Bible says this about another young person of good character: "I am always grateful for you. . . . I also remember the genuine faith of your mother Eunice. Your grandmother Lois had the same sort of faith, and I am sure that you have it as well. So I ask you to make full use of the gift that God gave you when I placed my hands on you. Use it well. God's Spirit doesn't make cowards out of us. The spirit gives us power, love, and self-control" (2 Tim. 1:3,5–7).

This is the essence of Christian character. Will you choose for yourself to honor God? It's both exciting and scary. Focus on the privilege. Then let God help you, as He did Ruth.

"Have self-control in everything" (Titus 2:6*b*).

DAY 2: HOW DOES HUMILITY HELP MY CHARACTER?

Humility is a right view of yourself and God. You recognize that God is God, and you're willing to let Him show you how to live life. You quietly do the right thing no matter who's looking. Far from being wimpy, humility is one of the most powerful qualities a Christian can possess.

But I do care about what people think. That's OK. Most of us do. Just be willing to let God give you courage to do right even if certain people think you're a goody-goody. The feelings are OK. Just let the right actions show. Let God heal you when you've been hurt by people you wanted to impress. And in the meantime, go ahead and do right. God says it like this: "If my own people will humbly pray and turn back to me and stop sinning, then I will answer them from heaven. I will forgive them and make their land fertile once again" (2 Chron. 7:14).

Decision by decision, seek God's face—meaning understand what He wants—and let Him show you what choice to make. Then obey. This is humility. This is character.

But I don't have any decisions right now. You don't decide today where to go to college or who to marry, but you do decide who to talk to and how to treat that person. Those choices are just as critical as the biggies. Each day lets you show whether you will honor God with your everyday actions or do the Sunday-only-put-on-an-act-when-people-are-watching thing.

"Too much pride can put you to shame. It's wiser to be humble" (Prov. 11:2).

DAY 3: HOW DOES CONSISTENCY HELP CHARACTER?

We like the scorekeeping method of pleasing God. That's the made-up view that as long as we have more goods than bads, we're OK in God's eyes. I can do a few bad things as long as I've just been on a missions trip, or if I go to church every Sunday. This view is OK on the good days, but even on the good days, it doesn't help much. Why? Because when you do wrong, even just a little bit of the time, it neutralizes the good. How easy is it to trust someone that lies just once? To tell a secret to someone who blabbed just once?

Work for consistent goodness, based in God's power. Picture what the world would be like if everyone obeyed God in these areas:

"Be sincere in your love for others. Hate everything that is evil and hold tight to everything that is good. Love each other as brothers and sisters and honor others more than you do yourself. Never give up. Eagerly follow the Holy Spirit and serve the Lord. Let your hope make you glad. Be patient in time of trouble and never stop praying. Take care of God's needy people and welcome strangers into your home. . . . Be friendly with everyone. Don't be proud and feel that you are smarter than others. . . . Don't let evil defeat you, but defeat evil with good" (Rom. 12:9–13,16,21).

As a woman of character, let your challenge consistently be to care, to tell the truth, and to work for peace. Be a person people can trust. Care for each person of whatever age and situation. The good you do by caring day after day will multiply for generations.

"Charm can be deceiving, and beauty fades away, but a woman who honors the Lord deserves to be praised" (Prov. 31:30).

DAY 4: HOW DO I KNOW WHAT'S RIGHT?

As you learn more about God each day, use a healthy dose of caution. If something doesn't seem right, it may not be right. This doesn't mean questioning all adults, but rather taking responsibility for the truths you learn and live. It's part of being a mature Christian who is responsible to God.

Two truths, equally important, bookend this process. First, you need Christians further down the Christian path to show you how to please God. Wise parents, caring teachers, and sensitive friends serve as these teachers. They give you a wealth of understanding described like this in the Bible:

"Now follow the example of the correct teaching I gave you, and let the faith and love of Christ Jesus be your model. You have been trusted with a wonderful treasure. Guard it with the help of the Holy Spirit, who lives within you" (2 Tim. 1:13–14).

The second truth is that false teachers will also come. The Bible warns about them repeatedly. Let the Bible and God's character help you evaluate everything you learn, even from believers. God will help you. Because you are a Christian, God has put within you His Holy Spirit to help you see and understand what is true and right:

"But Christ has blessed you with the Holy Spirit. Now the Spirit stays in you, and you don't need any teachers. The Spirit is truthful and teaches you everything. So stay one in your heart with Christ, just as the Spirit has taught you to do" (1 John 2:27).

Read the above verse cautiously. You don't have to go it alone. John was warning against false teachers, not all teachers. Balance this warning with the very wonderful parents, adults, and friends that God sends your way.

"My child, you must follow and treasure my teachings and my instructions. Keep in tune with wisdom and think what it means to have common sense" (Prov. 2:1,2).

DAY 5: WHERE DOES CHARACTER COME FROM?

Character comes as you imitate Jesus Christ. He Himself will give you the power to do this. In fact, He gave His blessing long ago:
"The Lord bless thee, and keep thee: The Lord make his face shine upon thee, and be gracious unto thee: The Lord lift up his countenance upon thee, and give thee peace" (Num. 6:24–26 KJV).

This blessing comes through your putting into practice what God says. God already blesses and keeps you; His face consistently watches over you; He's already gracious to you. You find His peace as you obey what He says. Live with the confidence that God is real, that God cares, and that each person matters to Him.

Why gossip about the person at the next lunch table when that person is precious to God? Find God's peace by speaking so well of every person that everyone knows they can trust you.

Why give up on learning a school subject when you know the God of the universe wants to work through you to make the best of the situation? Find God's peace through giving it your all and going to the people He sends.

Why assume any effort is useless, when everything you do influences other people? Even washing the dishes cheerfully can encourage your dad, who will encourage your brother, each of whom will consequently do better at work and school the next day.

Your character matters because the God of the universe is interested in you. He cares so much that He wants to help you squeeze every drop of good from this not-so-perfect life. So accept and live the blessing He's already given you—you're precious, and what you do matters.

"God's Spirit is in you and is more powerful than the one that is in the world" (1 John 4:4*b*).

7

WHY DOES MUTUALITY MATTER?

"Care about them as much as you care about yourselves" (Phil. 2:4).

DAY 1: WHAT IS MUTUALITY?

One of the most dangerous myths surrounding Christianity is that Christians are to do whatever anyone asks. This is seen as the kind thing, the "Christian" thing. But true Christianity works for the good of all persons. Letting people use you just won't accomplish that goal.

Instead work for God's good. Sometimes this means doing what another person asks. Other times it means guiding another person to do what you need. In both cases, work for right. Work toward mutuality, the togetherness that prompts each person to work for the good of all, the good God guides us to do. Mutuality enables you to solve your problems together rather than mooch off another, or let them mooch off you. Mutuality gives each person significance in each effort of life. The Bible says it this way:
"Care about them as much as you care about yourselves and think the same way that Christ Jesus thought" (Phil. 2:4–5).

Jesus was no doormat. He boldly said and did what needed saying and doing. When His disciples whined about feeding those who came to hear Jesus, He showed them how to use the food that was available (Luke 9:12–17). When people abused the temple by cheating good-hearted worshippers, Jesus turned over their tables and drove them out with a stern warning to stop (Mark 11:15–17). When an out-of-the-social-circle woman came to a gathering of prestigious church leaders, Jesus welcomed her warmly (Luke 7:36–50). When just-learning Peter correctly identified Jesus, Jesus affirmed him (Matt. 16:15–17).

What will it take to get people to do the right thing for the right reason? Give your efforts to that.

"You must encourage one another each day" (Heb. 3:13).

DAY 2: WHAT MAKES MUTUALITY?

Mutuality is togetherness. It begins with God and ends with God. Full togetherness can only happen when God is integral to it. Togetherness between two people is really a trio: you, your friend, and God. So weave your life most intimately with those most closely connected to God. These are not those who go to church most often, but those who honor God most consistently. Pick God-centered people for the guys you date, and for your closest friends.

A God-centered person shows that every action is an opportunity to honor God. Her words and attitudes bring a comfortable togetherness with every person encountered.

A God-centered person listens as well as speaks. He's as interested in receiving your insights and care as he is in giving them to you.

A God-centered person sees life as a pilgrimage, a continual learning about life and continual growing in understanding. She's open to new discoveries, but not so open-minded that her brains fall out.

A God-centered person is so comfortable with himself that he can focus fully on you. He doesn't have to prove himself or defend himself. He's free to make connections.

A God-centered person can do none of this alone, but grows mutuality with the help of Jesus. She allows Him to continually build in her a deepening comfort with self, an ever-improving self, a freedom to listen, and a focus on honoring God. The Bible Book of Job offers this picture of togetherness:

"Who placed the cornerstone, while morning stars sang and angels rejoiced?" (Job 38:6*b*–7).

"Fight a good fight for the faith and claim eternal life" (1 Tim. 6:11).

DAY 3: HOW CAN I FIND MUTUALITY?

In addition to being close to God, a giving person is willing to suffer and rejoice with you. It's not easy to find someone like this. Most friends stay while the going is good, but not too good. They stay for problems, as long as the problems demand nothing of them.

Find girlfriends and guy friends who are willing to weep with you without trying to make everything OK. They walk beside you as you move on to solutions. They know that sadness means people and events matter, not that you have no faith. These friends grieve with hope. And they allow you to grieve with them.

Find girlfriends and guy friends who rejoice with your successes. They don't have to one-up you by telling their stories of even greater triumph. They don't put themselves down with "I never win anything." Instead they move past jealousy to be genuinely happy with you. Then they invite you to be happy with them.

Such mutuality gives what the other person needs when they need it, and lets them give to you when you need it. The resources to do both come from God: "Praise God, the Father of our Lord Jesus Christ! The Father is a merciful God, who always gives us comfort. He comforts us when we are in trouble, so that we can share that same comfort with others in trouble. We share in the terrible sufferings for Christ, but also in the wonderful comfort he gives. We suffer in the hope that you will be comforted and saved" (2 Cor. 1:3–6*a*).

"You never disappoint us. You suffered as much as we did, and we know that you will be comforted as we were" (2 Cor. 1:7).

DAY 4: WHY IS MUTUALITY ROMANTIC?

What makes romance last? After being centered on God, it's mutuality. Mutual give-and-take provides the foundation love needs. Does he give to you as much as you give to him? Do you listen to him as much as he listens to you? Do you take turns picking where you'll go and how you'll spend money? Do you give and take comfortably and deliberately?

Certainly there are times he'll talk all evening, perhaps during a crisis. But if he does this constantly, interrupting whenever you try to tell your story, you don't yet have mutuality. Or if you demand he make all the plans, constantly going where you want to go, you've not reached mutuality.

Mutuality comes in finding guys who are already reasonably good at it. It's unlikely you can turn a piggish person into a giver merely through dating him. Nor can you take someone who refuses to receive and make him welcome your gifts. Giving and receiving are patterns that start in early childhood. Your efforts will help, so don't stop trying. But let your closest friendships and dating relationships be with those already versed in mutuality.

Romance grows through intentionally doing things that build oneness. The Bible recommends:

"But now you must stop doing such things. You must quit being angry, hateful, and evil. You must no longer say insulting or cruel things about others. And stop lying to each other. . . . God loves you and has chosen you as his own special people. So be gentle, kind, humble, meek, and patient" (Col. 3:8,9,12).

Love doesn't just happen. It grows through seeking to make the other person happy. It's a 100 percent–100 percent commitment in which both must give all. Lose yourself in mutually caring for the needs of each other.

"But all who do right will be rewarded with glory, honor, and peace, whether they are Jews or Gentiles" (Rom. 2:10).

DAY 5: ARE YOU TOO PIGGISH OR TOO PIOUS?

Most of us struggle with one side of mutuality. Some take too much. Others refuse to receive. The first is piggish. The second is overpious. Invite a parent and a trusted friend to evaluate your balance and suggest ways you might give more selflessly, and receive more gratefully. Then build mutuality:

•Grow giving by deliberately closing your mouth and listening avidly after asking a family member, "Tell me about your day."

•Learn to receive by telling about your day when someone invites it. Keep from whining by saying at least two positives for every negative.

•Grow giving by insisting that the other choose the activity of the evening. Enjoy yourself there rather than making it obvious that you're sacrificing.

•Learn to receive by choosing an activity that you really want to do, as long as it's not overexpensive or overdull to the other.

•Grow giving by focusing on personality, not the hunkdom scale. Though looks matter some, they are a low priority.

•Learn to receive by believing that the way you treat people is infinitely more important than how high you rank on the babedom scale. Like the way you look.

•Grow giving by liking guys as friends first, and then refusing to overlook your guy friends for potential romance. Your closest guy friend is frequently a great person to date.

•Learn to receive by noticing the way your girl-friends and guy friends already care about you. Thank God for this love.

•Give more and receive better by following these widely known but not as widely practiced words from the Bible:

"Treat others just as you want to be treated" (Luke 6:31).

8

HOW DOES EXCELLENCE BRING GOOD?

"When you eat or drink or do anything else, always do it to honor God"
(1 Cor. 10:31).

DAY 1: WHY DOES IT MATTER HOW I TREAT PEOPLE?

Because you are a believer, people watch you to see what Jesus is like. They see each of your actions as a living example of what God is all about. If you're cruel, they assume God must be judgmental. If you give more attention to certain people, they assume God plays favorites. If you act one way in church and another way in school, they assume God may have double standards.

Even when you don't mean to, and perhaps especially when you don't mean to, you portray a picture of God. Excellent treatment of people is perhaps the most powerful testimony possible. Will you be good and fair? Will you expect much while showing people how to meet those expectations? Will you share life with people as God does with you? The Bible says it like this:

"You are like a letter written by Christ and delivered by us. But you are not written with pen and ink or on tablets made of stone. You are written in our hearts by the Spirit of the living God. We are sure about all this. Christ makes us sure of the very presence of God. We don't have the right to claim that we have done anything on our own. God gives us what it takes to do all that we do. He makes us worthy to be the servants of his new agreement that comes from the Holy Spirit and not from a written Law. After all, the Law brings death, but the Spirit brings life" (2 Cor. 3:3–6).

What actions in you would God suggest to show that He is loving but not a pushover? That He offers both grace and demand? That He wants us to choose good behavior for happiness' sake? That He treasures each person?

"Don't let anyone make fun of you, just because you are young. Set an example for other followers by what you say and do, as well as by your love, faith, and purity" (1 Tim. 4:12).

DAY 2: WHY DOES IT MATTER WHAT I THINK?

Nobody knows my thoughts so why do they matter?

Thoughts lead to actions, which lead to habits, which lead to lifestyles.

C'mon! One little thought won't turn me into a death row criminal.

That's exactly the point.

What?

Stop your thoughts before they lead to actions; stop bad actions before they lead to habits; correct bad habits so they don't lead to piggish lifestyles.

Well, that's obvious!

Not always. Too many of us feed private thoughts that are ugly or selfish. Then we act them out as given permission by our inward schemes.

Like what?

Planning revenge against someone who hurt you. Then you spread a rumor that's just true enough to believe and cruel enough that people assume she's horrible.

I wouldn't do that.

Maybe not. But we all have thought sins that lead to action sins. Avoid any thoughts that are the opposite of:

"Whatever is true, pure, right, holy, friendly, and proper. Don't ever stop thinking about what is truly worthwhile and worthy of praise" (Phil. 4:8).

But I can't stop certain thoughts from coming into my head.

You're right. But you can keep them from staying there by replacing them with better thoughts. When those vengeful thoughts come, push them out by talking with God about how much her actions hurt you. Ask for grace to treat her well.

So there's no need to feel badly about bad thoughts. Just don't give them a home.

Right. Move them right on out of your head and out of your life.

"Your heart will always be where your treasure is" (Luke 12:34).

DAY 3: WHY DOES IT MATTER HOW I WORK?

Excellence is a powerful way to glorify God. When people see you do mundane tasks well, they are impressed by your motivation—God Himself. Too frequently Christians slack off since "God will bless it if He wants it to happen." Perhaps worse is the assumption that "school doesn't really matter—I focus on spiritual things like Bible studies and ministry." Both views reject the very real truth that God means for every act to be spiritual. Bible studies are not ends in themselves. They equip us to do school, work, friendship, and the other parts of real life. True spirituality is the way you honor God in daily life.

So do well whatever you do. When you approach school with dedication, you demonstrate that God cares about truth and knowledge. When you care for the people in your lunchroom, you show that ministry is for real life. When you give energy to your after-school job, you show that God loves the people you work for and the people you serve through your job. Excellence is life at its fullest and a tremendous demonstration of God's power. The Bible says it like this:

"Do your work willingly, as though you were serving the Lord himself, and not just your earthly master. In fact, the Lord Christ is the one you are really serving, and you know that he will reward you" (Col. 3:23–24).

If you don't do work and school well, you show that real life doesn't matter to God. In both school and work, show what God is like as you give it your best, solve your problems directly, and care for each person you encounter. If you fail to do these things, you deny God. You hurt His image.

"We wish that each of you would always be eager to show how strong and lasting your hope really is" (Heb. 6:11).

DAY 4: WHY DOES IT MATTER
HOW I TREAT MY FAMILY?

Real religion shows in how you treat the people you encounter every day. It's much easier to be polite to a stranger than to your brother who gets into your stuff. But showing kindness to your brother is where true faith shows. Why? Because it requires supernatural power. That power comes from God.

Just being a believer won't give you the power. You must plug into God's power source by choosing to talk calmly rather than yell. "Jamie, it makes me furious when you take my things without asking. Please ask. If you don't, I'll have to lock up my stuff." This is much better than "You shrimp! Get your dirty hands off my stuff!"

Then you work for real solutions, not just let your brother do whatever he wants. To let him just take your stuff would work against God's purposes. Your brother would assume he could treat people however he felt like treating them. He wouldn't learn mutuality, care for others, respect, or consideration. So agree on rules that give each of you the privacy and care you need. Invite your parents to help. The Bible says it like this:

"People who don't take care of their relatives, and especially their own families, have given up on their faith. They are worse than someone who doesn't have faith in the Lord" (1 Tim. 5:8).

Your family provides expressed kindness, respect, and interest in each others' lives. These daily actions provide an environment where your brother can grow much more willing to meet your needs, and where you can better meet his. Family is where spirituality hits the wheel.

"Kindness is rewarded—but if you are cruel, you hurt yourself" (Prov. 11:17).

DAY 5: HOW DOES EXCELLENCE GLORIFY GOD?

To glorify God is to draw positive attention to Him. Excellence draws attention to God because it stands out. We then see the goodness that is God. Examples:

•Excellent friends are those who carefully listen and respond with enthusiasm to whatever the speaker says. An excellent friend prods you to think about your choices without ever putting you down. An excellent friend feels sad with you and happy with you, and is willing to let you do the same with her. Such excellent friends stand out from the fair-weather, what-can-you-do-for-me, put-down kind of friend.

•Excellent students give full attention to classes, learning all they can with the time they have. They respect teachers, while evaluating what they say. Rather than swallow blindly, they taste to identify what God knows is right and true. These students worry less about grades than about learning. They stand out from students who get through class so they can move on to other things.

•Excellent family members take time to hear parents, sisters, brothers, and grandparents both to learn from and to teach them. These members know that good families require giving, so they invest there. These family members stand out from those who are defensive and lonely.

Where does God want you to become even more excellent? What happiness will you create when you do? The Bible says it like this:

"This message is certainly true. These teachings are useful and helpful for everyone. I want you to insist that the people follow them, so that all who have faith in God will be sure to do good deeds" (Titus 3:8).

"You do everything better than anyone else. You have stronger faith. You speak better and know more. You are eager to give, and you love us better. Now you must give more generously than anyone else" (2 Cor. 8:7).

9

WHAT IS MY VISION?

"Where there is no vision,
the people perish:
but he that keepeth the law,
happy is he"
(Prov. 29:18 KJV).

DAY 1: WHAT COULD HAPPEN IF . . . ?

What if . . . ?" is a wonderful life perspective. You see ways you can be better. You see ways to bring people together. You see ways to create happiness that lasts. Embrace the Scripture:
"It is truly wonderful when relatives live together in peace" (Psalm 133:1).

•What if people became color-blind and chose to get along with people of all cultures and races?
•What if families unselfishly encouraged each member to be her personal best, cheered with successes, supported through failures?
•What if school were fascinating?
•What if church members worked together?
•What if there were no war?
•What if cancer and disabilities were no more?

As you dream, see the good that can be. Then work to make it happen. Perhaps you become a medical researcher who cures hearing loss. Or you bridge friendships that bring oneness.

Both the dreaming and the making it happen must come in God's power and with God's guidance. Otherwise you could run the ship aground. The first part of the passage on the introductory page, "Where there is no vision the people perish" (Prov. 29:18), can also be translated "Without guidance from God law and order disappear" (CEV). God's visions give us a path to follow, a guide to go by. Without these we are aimless, confused, and lost. Lack of restraint appears freeing, but it's not. Without structure we don't know where to go.

Be a visionary. Let God show you the good that can be and then guide you to get there. You have the power to change the world.

"You are sure that you are a guide for the blind and a light for all who are in the dark" (Rom. 2:19).

DAY 2: CAN I BE A VISIONARY?

Absolutely. God explained that all people who receive Him receive His Holy Spirit. This Spirit brings dreams and visions that guide you to see and obey God:

"Later, I will give my Spirit to everyone. Your sons and daughters will prophesy. Your old men will have dreams, and your young men will see visions. In those days I will even give my Spirit to my servants, both men and women" (Joel 2:28–29).

This kind of vision is not for telling the future, or for knowing deep secrets that others can't know. Instead visions and dreams provide pictures of what God is like and how to serve Him. You share them with others for the purpose of encouraging each person to love and honor God.

Being a visionary can be lonely. Few people are willing to look clearly at the truth. Yet, when done with sensitivity, you can share visions in ways that whet people's appetites for more. "What if we had a school with no cliques?" "What if people who won elections were really qualified?" "What if we quit worrying about matching up and found friendships that freed us?"

The young-people-will-see-visions Scripture from Joel in the Old Testament was quoted in Acts 2:17–18 in the New Testament. The Holy Spirit had just visibly appeared to Jesus' followers to show everyone watching that God was alive, active, and working through the lives of His people. Today people can see through you that God is alive, active, and working through the lives of His people.

"Always set a good example for others" (Titus 2:7*a*).

DAY 3: HOW DO I SHARE WHAT I SEE?

People of vision are seldom popular people. But they are greatly loved. Why? Because they show in their actions what others seek—purpose, understanding, and confidence.

So when you see life as God means it to be, communicate it in the most powerful way—by living it. A prophet named Habakkuk showed how. He was troubled over the question of evil. Why did evil people take advantage of good ones? Why did good guys seem to finish last? God showed him that good guys may finish last, but they are the only ones who finish. As God revealed this truth to Habakkuk, He encouraged him to make it so clear that no one could miss it. The image is that of a billboard. And the best billboards are real people living the real truth:

"Then the Lord told me: 'I will give you my message in the form of a vision. Write it clearly enough to be read at a glance. At the time I have decided, my words will come true. You can trust what I say about the future. It may take a long time, but keep on waiting—it will happen! I, the Lord, refuse to accept anyone who is proud. Only those who live by faith are acceptable to me" (Hab. 2:2–4).

Faith is actually "faithfulness." As God explained to Habakkuk, active faithfulness to God does not always have immediate rewards, but it has definite rewards. The good will come. You can count on it. Show with your life, even if you are the only one who does, that honoring God is the way to go.

"No one lights a lamp and puts it under a bowl or under a bed. A lamp is always put on a lampstand, so that people who come into a house will see the light" (Luke 8:16).

DAY 4: WHAT IS AN ATTITUDE OF VISION?

Expectation. Confidence. Watchful waiting. All of these compose an attitude of vision. You know God is right, so you honor Him with certainty. Then you watch for the good that will come.

It's not easy, and yet it's tremendously easy. Honoring God basically means treating people like you would treat Jesus. Show interest. Compliment honestly. Encourage along the way. Meet needs quietly but definitely. Help everyone feel a part of things. Never put down, reject, or rank.

This is easy because people are where we live each day. It's hard because everything around us encourages otherwise. The ranking system in school is ridiculous but real. Lunch conversation spends more time on put-downs than affirmation of friendship. Competition between classmates can be bitter. Supposed friends leave people out of conversations, or directly degrade. And yet even in these circumstances, we can do the good and honorable thing. It happens best when just one other person is trying to do the same thing: "I [Jesus] promise that when any two of you on earth agree about something you are praying for, my Father in heaven will do it for you. Whenever two or three of you come together in my name, I am there with you" (Matt. 18:19–20).

Give your time to pursuits that bring good. Spend each moment like you'll never get it back, because you won't. And watch for God's good—sincere friendships; shared lives; uncomplicated successes.

"Faith makes us sure of what we hope for and gives us proof of what we cannot see" (Heb. 11:1).

DAY 5: WHAT IF NO ONE ELSE SEES WHAT I SEE?

As a visionary you may see things few other believers see. That can feel lonely. But you won't stay lonely. Why? Because God will show at least one other person the truth you see. It happened to Peter in Acts 10:

"But Peter took hold of him and said, 'Stand up! I am nothing more than a human.' As Peter entered the house, he was still talking with Cornelius. Many people were there, and Peter said to them, 'You know that we Jews are not allowed to have anything to do with other people. But God has shown me that he doesn't think anyone is unclean or unfit. . . . Now I am certain that God treats all people alike. God is pleased with everyone who worships him and does right, no matter what nation they come from" (Acts 10:26–28, 34b–35).

Peter found comradeship with Cornelius, a friend Peter would have previously rejected. Had he not followed the vision, Peter would have lost the good God planned for him and for Cornelius. But Peter did follow the vision. And you can too.

See and trust God's truth. Watch for the persons God sends to share your visions of truth. They might include a parent, a girlfriend, a guy friend, a boyfriend, even the one you newly treat with kindness. But it will always be someone. And it will always include God Himself.

Because God won't leave you alone, you can do the right thing. You can be a visionary, a person of character, a Christian. Why? Because He Himself will equip you. God will never leave you alone. Count on it.

"Descendants of Jacob, I, the Lord, created you and formed your nation. Israel, don't be afraid. I have rescued you. I have called you by name; now you belong to me" (Isa. 43:1).